First Biographies

Jesse Owens

by Eric Braun
Consulting Editor: Gail Saunders-Smith, PhD
Consultant: James E. Pinion, Board Member
Jesse Owens Memorial Park Board
Moulton, Alabama

Capstone
press
Mankato, Minnesota

Pebble Books are published by Capstone Press,
151 Good Counsel Drive, P.O. Box 669, Mankato, Minnesota 56002.
www.capstonepress.com

1 2 3 4 5 6 10 09 08 07 06 05

Library of Congress Cataloging-in-Publication Data
Braun, Eric, 1971–
    Jesse Owens / by Eric Braun.
    p. cm.—(Pebble books. First biographies)
    Includes bibliographical references and index.
    ISBN 0-7368-4230-6 (hardcover)
    1. Owens, Jesse, 1913–1980—Juvenile literature. 2. Track and field athletes—
United States—Biography—Juvenile literature. I. Title. II. Series: First biographies
(Mankato, Minn.)
GV697.O9B73 2006
796.42'092—dc22   2004029081

Summary: Simple text and photographs introduce the life of Jesse Owens, a track
and field athlete, who won four gold medals at the Olympics in 1936.

Note to Parents and Teachers

The First Biographies set supports national history standards for units on people and culture. This book describes and illustrates the life of Jesse Owens. The images support early readers in understanding the text. The repetition of words and phrases helps early readers learn new words. This book also introduces early readers to subject-specific vocabulary words, which are defined in the Glossary section. Early readers may need assistance to read some words and to use the Table of Contents, Glossary, Read More, Internet Sites, and Index sections of the book.

Table of Contents

Time Line

1913
born

Early Years

Jesse Owens was born in Alabama in 1913. His family did not have much money. Jesse was often sick.

◄ model of Jesse's childhood home at the Jesse Owens Park and Museum in Oakville, Alabama

Time Line

1913
born

1927
joins the
high school
track team

Jesse's family moved to Ohio when he was 9. In high school, Jesse joined the track team. He won many races and long jump events.

Jesse (center) winning a high school track race

Time Line

1913
born

1927
joins the
high school
track team

1933
attends Ohio
State University

Jesse's track coach taught him to work hard.
In college, Jesse broke three world records.
He also set a world record for the long jump.

Time Line

1913
born

10

1927
joins the
high school
track team

1933
attends Ohio
State University

1936
runs on U.S. Olymp
track team

Olympic Hero

In 1936, Jesse took part in the Olympic Games in Germany. Many athletes on the U.S. team were black.

Jesse (left) with U.S. Olympic teammates

Time Line

| 1913 born | 1927 joins the high school track team | 1933 attends Ohio State University | 1936 runs on U.S. Olymp track team |

Germany's leader, Adolph Hitler, believed that white people were better. He bragged that Germany's runners would beat the Americans.

◄ Adolph Hitler (center) at the 1936 Olympic Games

Time Line

●	●	●	☀
1913 born	1927 joins the high school track team	1933 attends Ohio State University	1936 runs on U.S. Olympic track team; wins four gold medals

14

But Hitler was wrong.
Jesse won four gold
medals. He broke two
Olympic records
and one world record.

Time Line

1913 born	1927 joins the high school track team	1933 attends Ohio State University	1936 runs on U.S. Olympic track team; wins four gold medals

After the Olympics

Many people treated Jesse like a hero when he came home. Some people treated him badly because he was black. Jesse could not find a job.

people cheering for Jesse at a parade

Time Line

1913	1927	1933	1936
born	joins the high school track team	attends Ohio State University	runs on U.S. Olympic track team; wins four gold medals

In 1950, Jesse finally
found a good job
giving speeches.
He told young people
how he worked hard
to become a great runner.

Jesse (left) speaking to a group of college students

1950
gets a job as a
public speaker

Time Line

1913
born

1927
joins the
high school
track team

1933
attends Ohio
State University

1936
runs on U.S. Olympic
track team; wins four
gold medals

In 1976, Jesse visited the White House. The president gave him the Medal of Freedom. Jesse died in 1980. People remember him as a great athlete.

1950
gets a job as a public speaker

1976
receives the Medal of Freedom award

1980
dies

Glossary

athlete—a person trained in a sport or game

event—one of the races or other activities at a sports competition; Jesse usually competed in the 100-yard dash, the 220-yard dash, and the long jump.

medal—a piece of metal shaped like a coin that an athlete receives for winning an event

Medal of Freedom—a medal the president gives to someone for their great works

Olympic Games—a competition of many sports events held every four years in a different country; people from around the world compete against each other.

record—the best time or length in an event

track—a sport that includes running and jumping in different events; track is also called track and field.

Read More

McKissack, Patricia, and Frederick McKissack. *Jesse Owens: Olympic Star.* Great African Americans. Berkeley Heights, N.J.: Enslow, 2001.

Monroe, Judy. *Jesse Owens: Track-and-Field Champion.* Mankato, Minn.: Capstone Press, 2005.

Sutcliffe, Jane. *Jesse Owens.* On My Own Biography. Minneapolis: Carolrhoda Books, 2001.

Internet Sites

FactHound offers a safe, fun way to find Internet sites related to this book. All of the sites on FactHound have been researched by our staff.

Here's how:

1. Visit *www.facthound.com*

2. Type in this special code **0736842306** for age-appropriate sites. Or enter a search word related to this book for a more general search.

3. Click on the **Fetch It** button.

FactHound will fetch the best sites for you!

23

Index

Word Count: 200
Grades: 1–2
Early-Intervention Level: 18

Editorial Credits
Katy Kudela, editor; Heather Kindseth, set designer; Patrick D. Dentinger, book designer;
    Kelly Garvin, photo researcher/photo editor

Photo Credits
Corbis/Bettmann, 1, 8, 10, 16; Hulton-Deutsch Collection, 12; Jerry Cooke, 20
Getty Images Inc./Hulton Archive, 14; Hulton Archive/New York Times Co., 6;
    Time Life Pictures/James Burke, 18; Topical Press Agency, cover
Joyce Cole, 4